PUNS-A-POPPIN'
Original Punbits, Punecdotes, and Punzles

by

Tyler Kaus

Illustrations by Tony Couch

DORRANCE PUBLISHING CO., INC.
PITTSBURGH, PENNSYLVANIA 15222

All Rights Reserved
Copyright © 2001 by Tyler Kaus
No part of this book may be reproduced or transmitted
in any form or by any means, electronic or mechanical,
including photocopying, recording, or by any information
storage and retrieval system without permission in
writing from the publisher.

ISBN # 0-8059-5309-4
Printed in the United States of America

First Printing

For information or to order additional books, please write:
Dorrance Publishing Co., Inc.
643 Smithfield Street
Pittsburgh, Pennsylvania 15222
U.S.A.
1-800-788-7654
Or visit our web site and on-line catalog at
www.dorrancepublishing.com

Dedication

To Richard Lederer—
the punmeister and master of word play,
whose books were my main inspiration
to publish my own original
punbits, punecdotes, and punzles.

PREFACE

Most everyone has heard the pronouncement of John Dennis, who declared that "**A pun is the lowest form of wit.**" And, after hearing a pun that he intensely disliked, he also said "**A man who could make so vile a pun would not scruple to pick a pocket.**"

It seems that many people feel strongly about the worth, or lack thereof, of the so-called art of punning. Here are some of the more interesting comments on the value of puns—many of which emanate from very famous persons, not a few of whom are literary giants:

A good pun may be admitted among the small excellencies of lively conversation.
— *James Boswell*

If a pun is the lowest form of wit, it is, therefore, the foundation of all wit.
— *Henry Erskine*

In the beginning was the pun.
— *Samuel Beckett*

The assumption that puns are <u>per se</u> contemptible, betrayed by the habit of describing every pun not as 'a pun,' but as 'a bad pun' or 'a feeble pun,' is a sign at once of sheepish docility and a desire to seem superior. Puns are good, bad, and indifferent, and only those who lack the wit to make them are unaware of the fact.
— *Henry Fowler*

Hanging is too good for a man who makes puns. He ought to be drawn and quoted.
— *Fred Allen*

On the making of puns: One must strike while the irony is hot.
— *Phyllis McGinley*

A pun is not bound by the laws which limit nicer wit. It is a pistol let off at the ear, not a feather to tickle the intellect.
— *Charles Lamb*

A truly clever pun is a work of art.
— *James J. Kilpatrick*

Of puns it has been said that those who most dislike them are least able to utter them.
— *Edgar Allan Poe*

I love puns so much that my wife made a sign I hang over my desk: CAUTION! INCORRIGIBLE PUNSTER. PLEASE DON'T INCORRIGE.
— *Bob Trowbridge*

I should be punished
For every pun I shed:
Do not leave a puny shred
Of my punnish head!
— *Dr. Samuel Johnson*

A good punster has to either keep puffin' along or go loony when people are robin him of his fun.
— *John Rizzo*

Punsters' minds work like Las Vegas one-armed bandits, with plums and cherries and oranges spinning madly upon someone's utterance, searching for the right combination to connect on a pun.

— *Robert Greenman*

A quotation, like a pun, should come unsought, and then be welcomed only for some propriety or felicity justifying the intrusion.

— *Robert William Chapman*

A pun is the lowest form of humor...when you don't think of it first.

— *Oscar Levant*

Science has not found a cure for the pun.

— *Robert Byrne*

Punning is a talent which no man affects to despise, but he who is without it.

— *Jonathan Swift*

A pun is language on vacation.
> — *Christopher Morley*

Never point a pun at a friend. It might be loaded. Besides, you might kill a pun pal.
> — *John Crosbie*

...something every person belittles and everyone attempts.
> — *Louis Untermeyer*

There is no such thing as a female punster. I guess that means that punning is a crime for malefactors only!
> — *Oliver Wendell Holmes*

Language play is the new frontier of English.
> — *Don L. F. Nilsen*

...plurality of reference is in the very nature of language, and its management and exploitation is one of the joys of writing.
> — *Anthony Burgess*

The pun has been said to be the lowest form of humus—earthly wit that everyone digs…. If someone complains that punning is the lowest form of humor, you can tell them that poetry is verse.
— *John Crosbie and Bob Davies*

…a joke based on the infirmities of language.
— *Leonard L. Levinson*

The seeds of Punning are in the minds of all men, and tho' they may be subdued by Reason, Reflection, and good Sense, they will be very apt to shoot up in the greatest Genius, that is not broken and cultivated by the rules of Art.
— *Joseph Addison*

Punning may be the lowest, but at all events is the most harmless kind of wit, because it never excites envy.
— *Samuel Taylor Coleridge*

Puns are the wit of words. They are exactly the same to words which wit is to ideas, and consist in the sudden discovery of relations in language.

—*Sidney Smith*

…a low species of wit.

— *Noah Webster*

People that make puns are like wanton boys that put coppers on railroad tracks. They amuse themselves and other children, but their little trick may upset a freight train of conversation for the sake of a battered witticism.

— *Oliver Wendell Holmes*

…to torture one poor word ten thousand ways.

— *John Dryden*

A pun's the lowest form of wit,
It does not tax the brain a bit;
One merely takes a word that's plain
And picks one out that sounds the same.

— *Anonymous*

...two strings of thought tied with an acoustic knot

— *Arthur Koestler*

Punning is an art of harmonious jingling upon words, which, passing in at the ears, excites a titillary motion in those parts; and this, being conveyed by the animal spirits into the muscles of the face, raises the cockles of the heart.

— *Jonathan Swift*

...a noble thing per se. It fills the mind, it is a perfect sonnet; better.

— *Charles Lamb*

Puns are little "plays on words" that a certain breed of person loves to spring on you and then look at you in a certain self-satisfied way to indicate that he thinks that you must think that he is by far the cleverest person on Earth now that Benjamin Franklin is dead, when in fact what you are thinking is that if this person ever ends up in a lifeboat, the

other passengers will hurl him overboard by the end of the first day even if they have plenty of food and water.
— *Dave Barry*

...form of wit, to which wise men stoop and fools aspire.
— *Ambrose Bierce*

Le calembour est la fiente de l'espirit qui vole. (Puns are droppings of soaring wits.)
— *Victor Hugo*

I am a surgeon to old shoes; when they are in great danger I recover them.
— A shoemaker in *Julius Caesar*
— (one of some 1062 plays on words written by William Shakespeare)

A paltry, humbug just; those who have the least wit make them best.
— *William Combe*
(Does that put Shakespeare on the witless list?)

INTRODUCTION

I started making up puns at about age seven, inspired in part, by my Uncle Gabe Ondeck, who cracked a pun just about every time he talked to me. So, I learned to crack back, feeble as my efforts were at that time.

Later, in high school, I played word games with Dudley Vernon, a fellow student. Original word play soon became a favorite hobby of mine.

At Duke University, I majored in English, naturally. After graduation, I joined a New York City ad agency where I wrote advertising copy and edited magazines for 43 years. Of course, I managed to work an original pun into a lot of my headlines.

Throughout my advertising career, I became increasingly infatuated with the books of Richard Lederer, who was an expert in the field of all kinds of word play, particularly puns. I have bought all of his books (15 when I last counted), and they swiftly turned me on even stronger to come up with puns of my own. His books that inspired me most were: *The Play of Words, Pun and Games*, and *Get Thee To a Punnery*. I recommend all of them to everyone who loves this marvelous, crazy language of ours.

Although there are many different styles of pun construction, as wonderfully described by Mr. Lederer, the puns in this book of mine are basically of two general types: short ones (punbits) and longer ones (punecdotes). I have not separated these two types, thinking it might be more fun to mix them up for a more varied reading experience.

You probably already know that some puns can be extremely clever, others hilarious, and often, a combination of both. Hopefully, you'll enjoy all of these forms in this book.

One last thought: I firmly believe that every pun in this book is my own original concoction. If, however, any of them are similar to others that have been printed, I assure you it was not intended. If there are some here like that, I'm sure Mr. Lederer will tell me about it! Remember, the more you groan at these puns, the more successful they are.

PUNBITS, PUNECDOTES, AND PUNZLES

A gorgeous beauty queen, who posed for fashion ads before getting injured in a skiing accident, dedicated her life to visiting hospital and rehab centers in her wheelchair. There she was an inspiration to newly injured kids. She was truly a **roll model**.

• • •

A pair of cormorants, perched next to each other on the tips of a tree branch just above the surface of the lake, were waiting for fish to swim by. The male cormorant, periodically, whisked his broad tail in the water, to attract fish, which would think the droplets were bugs. In the process, he scattered the droplets, showering his mate, which was perched just behind him. A naturalist, observing this procedure, called it "**Tailbaiting**."

• • •

A very loud and abusive, mentally defective defendant was not allowed in the courtroom at his trial. The judge ruled that as far as a court appearance was concerned, the defendant was not **fit to be tried**.

• • •

A very old man married a very young woman, both of whom were multi-millionaires. They argued constantly over who had the most money. That, and their great age disparity, made for a most unpleasant ongoing relationship. All of which proves that **famillionarity breeds chrontempt**.

• • •

What does a joke lover like most about Easter morning? **Hot cross puns**.

• • •

When the Botany teacher asked his students to each bring in a daisy for flower analysis, one lazy, often-forgetful student named Calvin shuffled into class late without his flower. The teacher said, "It figures, You **lack a daisy, Cal.**"

• • •

What's a stork's favorite cold-weather drink? A **hot toady**.

• • •

What's the favorite, inexpensive game of Glasgow's young frogs? **Hop Scotch**.

• • •

A woman was having difficulty talking because a pit from the cherry pie she was eating had gotten stuck in her throat. You might say that her throat was **occlu-pie-d**.

• • •

Morton O'Brien, a mail carrier in Kansas nearing retirement, was planning to return to his hometown in Ireland. There he wished to be buried in the family plot when the time came. Unfortunately, he died before he had retired. His good friends in Kansas, knowing of his wish to return to Ireland, took up a collection, packed his coffin in dry ice, and mailed Morton's remains back to his hometown. The headline in the local newspaper about this unusual event was "Mailman O'Brien gets **post-Morton** sendoff!"

• • •

A very expensive, gourmet restaurant hired an attractive American Indian named Autumn Songbird as their hostess. For a while, the management was very pleased with her performance. However, gradually she developed an attitude, and she was not as gracious as the job called for. The owner of the restaurant was afraid to fire her because she represented a minority and might very well sue him for discrimination because of her race. Imagine how happy the owner was one day when Autumn announced that she had accepted another job elsewhere! So happy was he, that when she walked out of the restaurant's front door for the last time, he cranked up his stereo system to play "**Autumn Leaves.**"

• • •

A man and woman robber team, released together from a Kansas jail, decided to get married. After the ceremony, since there was no rice handy, their criminal buddies threw corn kernels at the couple as they made a dash for their stolen honeymoon car. One of their friends remarked, as he threw a handful of kernels, "There goes **corn with the sinned.**"

• • •

Patient to his psychiatrist: I'm worried, Doc. Last night I found myself in a horrible nightmare. I dreamed I was in an awful country ruled by Satan and that country was actually Hades. What does that mean?

<u>Shrink</u>: Well, first of all, you weren't in a nightmare. It was actually a **HellLucifernation**.

• • •

<u>Roommate #1</u>: Don't you ever get tired of listening to that Vivaldi tape?

<u>Roommate #2</u>: That's not Vivaldi, it's Telemann.

<u>Roommate #1</u>: How about a little Beethoven or Mozart for a change?

<u>Roommate #2</u>: Get a life! Those guys are way overrated, and the classical music stations play 'em to death.

<u>Roommate #1</u>: Do me a favor, will you? **If it ain't baroque, don't nix it.**

• • •

An old retired sailor, pretending to be a multimillionaire, committed bigamy and married a rich young lady solely for her money. The local gossip columnist headlined the story "**The Crime of the Ancient Marrier.**"

• • •

My friend Malcolm was in a very bad mood, complaining that his back was very painful. I suggested he go to a chiropractor for an adjustment. He took my advice, but when I saw him again a little later, he was in an even worse mood and said his back hurt him even more than before. I had to agree with this **Malcolmtent** that he was indeed **Maladjusted.**

• • •

Many years ago in China, a large number of sheep had contracted a very contagious disease. The Chinese were forced to put the infected sheep to sleep, which greatly reduced their flocks. This practice came to be known as **ewethinAsia.**

• • •

Q. How did the very zealous feminist react when she read the second chapter of Paul's epistle in I Timothy, which trashed the woman's role in the church?
A. She was **apPaulled**.

• • •

Sue was watching a video with her boyfriend Tom at his parents' house, when one of the actors began using some very profane language. She grabbed her head and exclaimed "Ow! Language like that gives me a splitting headache!" Tom asked Sue if she wanted an aspirin, whereupon she leaned forward and yelled "Boo!" at the TV set. "There," she said. "No more headache! You see, Tom, whenever my head hurts from hearing sacrilegious language, I've got something that's a whole lot better than aspirin: **I-boo-profane**."

• • •

A SPLIT-REVERSAL CLICHÉ PUNECDOTE

An apprentice chef in an upscale Oriental restaurant, after making a batch of tempura, accidentally spilled some tea into his creation. The head chef became enraged, but he soon calmed down because he realized that the entire affair was just **a tea-pest in a temp-pot.**

• • •

A Dutch cheesemeister was giving one of his pupils a lesson on how to make a unique kind of cheese that he had invented. He stressed the fact that if it is not made right, it will become overpoweringly smelly. The secret was to be sure to ladle off every bit of the surface liquid before letting the cheese harden—otherwise, there would be a smelly mess. "In other words," he warned his pupil, "it's **stink or skim.**"

• • •

Article in a small-town newspaper: "Several patients of Dr. Reuben Jones are recovering slowly from severe stomach pains as a result of ingesting a 'snake oil' concoction made in Dr. Jones' basement. Dr. Jones has previously been questioned by health authorities about some of his questionable practices." Headline for this story: "Local Doctor Just **What He's Quacked Up to Be.**"

• • •

When a genetic scientist cross-bred two different types of exotic rabbits, the result was a weird, ferocious animal that nearly bit off his scalp. He found it to be a truly **hare-raising experience**.

• • •

What carol did the housewife sing when she saw, with dismay, a large pile of dust under her bed? **"Sigh Lint Site."**

• • •

What do you call the medical condition in which the front ends of the feet "go to sleep" for a long period of time? **Coma-toes.**

• • •

A farmer had a bunch of cattle that sometimes got into trouble by straying into areas of quicksand and mud on his ranch. Occasionally, a steer would die when it couldn't get out of the quicksand. Twice as often, he would lose a steer in the boggy area. He concluded that **a herd in the sand is worth two in the mush.**

• • •

Once a year, on the anniversary of the day he retired, a Shakespearean actor officiated at a ceremonial family dinner. The main course was a giant Virginia ham, over which he poured a bottle of fine cognac and set it ablaze. While it was burning, he recited the famous "To be or not to be" soliloquy. The family referred to this histrionic performance as the annual **Hamlit** ceremony.

•••

What do you call a faux emerald shaped like a clover? A **sham-rock**.

•••

What do you call two mallards that hate water? A **paradox**.

•••

What's the name of a special art gallery that only displays old sculptures, photos and drawings of cats? A **mew-see-em**.

•••

The story goes that when the "Magic Slate" was first invented, the inventors demonstrated it to a group of "money men" to convince them to finance its manufacture and promotion. One of the inventors made a few marks on the "Slate," lifted up the top transparent sheet, put it back down, and saw that the sheet was now blank. After repeating this demonstration a few times, one of the prospective backers exclaimed, "Amazing! You mean to say that you can make marks on that slate over and over again?"

"Yes," said one of the inventors. "There is virtually no limit to how many times you can make marks on the 'Magic Slate'."

A second investor piped up, "That is indeed **remarkable!**"

● ● ●

When the new restaurant was about to open, the two owners debated on whether or not to have music playing during the dining hours — what kind it should be, and how loud. One of the owners said, "After we open, let's play a different kind of music each week, and also try it at different volume levels. And during this trial period, let's get the customers' opinions on what they prefer."

"Oh," said the other owner, "You mean, **play it by ear**."

•••

What do you call the noises made by a gambler who bets his bankroll on one last roll of the dice in hopes his "ship will come in" — only to discover that his "ship" foundered and sank? **Crapsighs**.

•••

What do you call it when a group of U-boats come together to form a tightly grouped underwater attack team? **Submerge**.

•••

When a big bird in the zoo that looks like an emu acts up and needs to be disciplined, what happens to it? It gets **ostrichsized**.

•••

What's the title of the song about a guy in Dallas immersed in the painful financial process of meeting the April 15th deadline? **"Steeped in the hurt of taxes."**

• • •

What is a simple way of defining a group of uncouth males who make disturbances at a party and then overstay their welcome? **Rude-a-men-tarry**.

• • •

What do you call an undertaker who has the unique talent of being able to put a smile on the face of a deceased that stays fixed? The **grin keeper**.

• • •

What do you call a lumberjack who doesn't drink? A **treetotaler**.

• • •

What do you call a bashful songbird that slyly appropriates food stolen by other birds? A **shylark**.

• • •

Soon after a man had consumed a huge amount of a popular food made from soy beans, he came down with a strange case of influenza. This resulted in his toes becoming very swollen. He was diagnosed as having **toeflu**.

• • •

What do you call it when you experience a desire to scratch a rash caused by the simultaneous consumption of whisky and a popular black confection? **Liquoritch**.

• • •

That condo is so small, you could call it a **condominimum**.

• • •

Helen, the daughter of a Native American couple by the name of Highwater, was a very headstrong child. One day, while she was playing outside in the rain, her father called to her to come inside the teepee. She pretended she didn't hear him. Exasperated, her father shouted to her, "**Come Helen Highwater**, or I'll thrash your hide!" (Thus was born another popular phrase into our language.)

• • •

How come so many kids today are getting various parts of their body pierced? Well, when their friends are all doing it, they feel pressured to do it, too. You could call it **pierce pressure**.

• • •

What do you call it when a person has a strong compulsion to "explode" every word or phrase he sees or hears into a pun? **Punnel fission**.

• • •

PUN-NIOR:

A man who lost both arms and legs in a one-car accident sued the manufacturer of the car for his injuries, claiming that the car was defective. The defense lawyer, summing up his case in court said, "Ladies and gentlemen of the jury, I believe we have proven that the car was not defective. Don't let the plaintiff's **disarming** appearance swing your decision. In fact, he really **doesn't have a leg to stand on.**"

• • •

The initiation procedure for a college fraternity was to collect a number of items via a treasure hunt. To make the task even harder, the names of the items desired were hidden in clues. One of the treasure hunters had solved all the clues and collected all the items — all, that is, but one. He went to the organizer of the hunt and said, "There's just one clue I'm having trouble with, but I think I may have solved it. I believe it is 'two honey bees.' Can you tell me if this is right? The organizer replied, "I'm sorry, that would be against the rules. All I can say is, **two bees or not two bees, that is the quest, son.**"

• • •

<u>Save the Dollpuns</u>
A little Tibetan girl worshipped her stuffed toy animal from Peru so much that she called it her **Dolly Llama**.

When the little girl's brother, Salva, ripped up her favorite Barbie doll in the modern-art museum, she screamed to her mother, "**Salva tore dolly!**"

What would you call a Broadway musical featuring themes of deception and one-on-one sword fights? "**Guise and Duels.**"

• • •

Did you really make that big boat out of the wood in that old pier? Yes. It's **a ship off the 'ol dock**.

•••

It takes a lot of skill to deliberately lose at golf to your boss (who is a very sore loser), and make it look like you really tried to win. For example, it is hard to miss a short putt by stroking the ball so that it rims the cup without falling in. This art form could be summed up as **"The goof of the putting is in the cheating."**

•••

What is the motto under which a society of canine cannibals operates? **Dog Eat Dog.**

•••

There is a popular Japanese restaurant that features stir-fry vegetables and egg rolls, with rock-and-roll music playing on the sound system. What do you think they call it? **Wok 'N Roll.**

•••

A physician back in the early 1900s, who visited his patients via horse and carriage moonlighted as both an undertaker and an exterminator in order to make ends meet. He was known locally as the **hearse and buggy doctor**.

• • •

Even though his patient with laryngitis had been scheduled to be examined ahead of his cardiac patient, the doctor decided to see them in reverse order. That's because he believed in **putting the heart before the hoarse.**

• • •

What do you call it when a psychiatrist convenes a bunch of mentally and emotionally disturbed patients, with the treatment consisting of one-on-one grabbing and gazing intently into each other's eyes? **Grope stare-apy.**

• • •

Once **apun** a time, a stubborn old woman was so old-fashioned that she always wore clothes just like her grandmother used to wear, including a laced-up corset and a horrible 1890s-style wig. She hated anything "modern," so she weighed the candy she sold in her store on a dilapidated old balance scale. She was known in the neighborhood as **clothes-minded, straight-laced, wig-headed, and set-in-her-weighs**.

• • •

First teenager: Whaddaya say we go bowling tonight?
Second teenager: I can't. Gonna be tied up tonight, doing a little S & M with my girlfriend.
First teenager: Wow! I didn't know you were into that kinky stuff!
Second teenager: Whaddaya mean, kinky stuff?
First teenager: You know. S & M.
Second teenager: It's not what you think. We're just going out for **Supper and a Movie**.

• • •

What do you call what David could have done to his enemy, King Saul, when the latter was squatting in the cave where David was hiding? An **asSault**.

• • •

A young man, recuperating from a broken right leg and a sprained left ankle, came to his doctor's office walking very slowly with a walker. He asked the doc if he thought it would be okay for him to "graduate" to a pair of Canadian crutches, the kind that give support through the arms rather than the shoulders. After examining the patient thoroughly and thinking about it for a few minutes, the doctor said, "Well, if I had to bet on your success with the Canadians at this stage in your recuperation, I'd have to say it's a fifty-fifty chance you'll be able to manage with them. To put it another way, it's strictly **crutch and go**."

• • •

A newlywed bride complained to her mother that, for some reason, the tea she fixed at dinnertime didn't seem to taste as good as when she made it at other times. When her mother found out that she <u>first</u> boiled the water and put in the tea leaves, and <u>then</u> prepared the dinner, she said to her daughter, "Remember when you were a little girl, and I told you to carefully look before you leap across the road? Well, your tea problem is similar. In this case, you should **cook before you steep**."

• • •

When a teenage boy with beautiful blonde locks announced that he shaving his head bald so he could join a local gang of skinhead toughs, his mother wailed, **"Hair today, goon tomorrow!"**

• • •

Did you hear about the man so worried about his accelerating baldness that he spent hours each day arranging his remaining hair to cover his receding hairline, and using hair-restoring pills and tonics? He became so confused that he **didn't know if he was combing or growing**.

• • •

A 300-pound football player went to a costume party dressed in a giant-sized lion suit. But, while he was helping himself at the buffet table, he accidentally knocked over a bowl of vichyssoise, which soaked the long, flowing hair on the back of his lion suit. One of the guests remarked, "Look! There goes **Soupermane!**"

• • •

What satisfaction do mountain climbers derive form scaling high peaks? The **feeling of acclimbishment**.

• • •

A famous actor was in the recording studio supervising the mixing of his new movie. While the music was being added to the voice and sound effects tracks, he shouted to the engineer, "No! That music is all wrong for this scene! If we must have music here, use something from Vivaldi or Telemann. In other words, guys, **if it ain't baroque, don't mix it!**"

•••

A huge man with a 60-inch waist told the clerk of a Hawaiian surf shop that he wanted to rent a surfboard for the day. The clerk said that the waves were too high for a man of his size to surf today, and that a large man had tried it last year under similar conditions and been killed. Mr. Large said, "That's my problem. Will you or won't you rent me a board? Yes or No?"

"No," said the clerk. So, Mr. Large walked out of the shop.

Another customer who had overheard all this said to the clerk, "Well, that proves it — **a word to the wide is surf-ficient.**"

•••

<u>Woman</u>: Don't get me wrong. I hate cannibals as much as anyone. But, what the circus is doing this year is so outrageous that I'm not subjecting my kids to such a perverted spectacle!
<u>Man</u>: Whatever do you mean?
<u>Woman</u>: Haven't you heard? The circus is actually advertising that it is featuring **shooting a human cannibal** at every performance!

● ● ●

What do you call a guy who puts every box of corn flakes he buys into his refrigerator? A **cereal chiller**.

● ● ●

A man was having breakfast in an Amtrak dining car when he heard a voice belting out a familiar song from the kitchen compartment. He asked the waiter who it was, and the waiter said: "Oh, that's the cook. Every time he makes hash, he does his parody of Gene Kelly in that famous musical."

Just then, the diner heard the words soaring from the kitchen, "I'm happy again…**slingin' in the train!**"

• • •

After getting badly cut and bruised while on his school's boxing team, the student decided to give up boxing and switch to wrestling. This prompted his father to quip, **"A grapple a day keeps the sock-ter away."**

• • •

Everybody knows that Walt Disney's famous rodent, Mickey, had only one girlfriend, Minnie. That's why Mickey could be called **"monoga-mouse."**

• • •

A man who is particularly adept at fixing motors of all kinds, no matter how intricate the problem, could be said to possess a great deal of **enginuity**.

•••

A couple named their daughter after their favorite singer, Dinah Shore. But, unlike the singer's cheery personality, their daughter was morose and had a fiery, explosive temper. So, when a new babysitter arrived one evening to take care of Dinah and was told of this trait, the sitter was concerned and asked the parents, "If I stop her from doing something she ought not to do, will she have a fit and blow up?"

The father answered, "Knowing our daughter as we do, I must admit, **Dinah might**."

•••

While rotating German sausages on the barbecue spit, the host of the party tripped and fell into the grill, burning himself severely. When one of his guests phoned the hospital to ask the nurse about his condition, she replied, "He's not doing so well right now. He **took a turn for the wurst**."

• • •

When the parents returned from an evening out, they asked their babysitter how their little boy behaved. The exasperated sitter replied, "I never **sausage** a brat! He's **the wurst!**"

• • •

When asked about the condition of the crate of sausages that fell off the forklift at the loading dock, the foreman replied, "I'm afraid it's a **wurst-case scenario.**"

• • •

A very proper lady was embarrassed by a number of her husband's crude and uncouth actions. The one she most objected to was his habit of rapping thunderously on the doors of people they visited. One day, when they were delivering a gift of sausage to a German couple, her husband repeated his performance of crashing his fist against the neighbors' door. That was the last straw. She pushed away his hand and said, "In all my life, I have never seen such a crude display of bad manners! No doubt about it, **you knock wurst!**"

• • •

A Humane Society employee observed a collarless, flea-infested puppy that was furiously scratching itself on Mr. Brown's lawn. When she asked Mr. Brown if the dog belonged to him, he answered indignantly, "I hate dogs! And that miserable mutt is certainly **not my pup of fleas**!"

• • •

A church deacon went to a real estate agent to rent a golf course for a weekend fund-raising tournament in order to help with the church's new building project. But, the rent was so high that he was delighted when one of his friends knew of a course near the Everglades in Florida that the church could use for free. So, the deacon booked it, site unseen. When he went to check out the course a week before the tournament, he was horrified to discover that some of the fairways were underwater! The lesson here is: **Never book a gift course in the South**.

•••

In 1849, a prospector located an area in California that had all the earmarks of a rich gold lode. When he went to the Land Office to stake his claim, he found out that someone had already claimed the entire area. It was **out of site, out of mine**.

•••

In France, a motorist's automobile lost power and was just barely able to make it to a filing station at a snail's pace. The mechanic, who didn't speak much English, looked under the hood, made a few adjustments and nodded to the driver, who asked him if he had fixed the problem. The mechanic smiled and said, **"Yes. Cargo."**

• • •

A teenage boy, on a very hot summer's day, noticed three kids in a canoe out of control in a fast-moving river. He knew that a big waterfall just ahead would surely kill the kids if they went over it. So, he jumped into the raging water, swam out to the canoe, and pulled it ashore just as it was about to plummet over the falls. When the press found out about the lad's heroic deed, they were just as impressed with how humble and modest he was about what he had done. Next morning, the headline in the local paper read: **"It Was Not Just the Feat, But the Humility."**

• • •

An emergency-room physician was examining a man who was brought in suffering from convulsions. As the fit was subsiding, he found out that the patient was not an epileptic, was not taking any drugs or medications, and was not allergic to any foods except raw eggs, to which he was violently allergic. Probing further, the doctor discovered that the man had recently eaten a fancy salad in an upscale restaurant. When he found out what kind of salad it was, he said, "My prescription for your problem is to avoid those **seizure salads**."

• • •

When a young lady's father found out she was pregnant, he forced her boyfriend to marry her by literally attending the wedding with a loaded shotgun. The young man really didn't want to get married, but he said philosophically, "**Easier wed than dead**."

• • •

A lady rushed to get to a department store that was having a huge sale on handbags. She was held up in traffic and arrived thirty minutes after the store had opened. When she got to the handbag sale counter, the clerk told her that all the bags had been sold. He said, "You know that famous Leo Durocher quote, 'Nice guys finish last?' Well, here at this store we have a slightly different saying, **'Nice buys diminish fast.'"**

• • •

One of the prisoners in Cell Block A had been bullying and abusing his fellow inmates to such an extent that they decided to do something about it. They ganged up on him and beat him up — all the while gleefully cheering with each blow. When a guard heard the commotion and saw the guy covered with cuts, welts, and bruises, he said, "I see you guys have been having quite a **cellabrasion!**"

• • •

What do you call a weird, puzzling percussion instrument that has two heads and is played by two inhabitants of a convent? A **conundrum**.

• • •

What do you call a man who constantly eats garlic and loves to tell puns? A **pungent**.

•••

What do you call a large book on etiquette that thoroughly covers every aspect of proper human conduct and decorum? A **fine couth tome**.

•••

What do you call it when the pitcher and the batter get into a fist fight, and both teams' benches join the fray? **Basebrawl**.

•••

An amateur inventor put together a combination of ingredients in the form of a solid rod, which had the ability to immediately produce a bronze color when rubbed against the skin. He asked his brother, an ad man, to come up with a catchy name for this amazing tanning rod. The result: **TanFastStick**. They believed that they would make a fortune with this revolutionary new product. But they didn't. **Un-fortune-ately**.

• • •

A moonshiner got tired of making frequent trips to town to deliver his illegal booze in quart bottles, which he hid under the front seat of his car. So, he poured his "still-fresh" gin into wooden barrels, loaded them into a coffin, and began making his deliveries in an old hearse. On one of his trips to town, he was stopped by the sheriff for a broken tail light. The old hearse made the sheriff curious, and when he looked inside, he discovered the barrels of gin inside the coffin. Later, as the sheriff was locking up the moonshiner in the county jail, he said, "I guess no one ever told you: **'Don't put all your kegs in one casket!'**"

• • •

Rebecca, a *Notorious* but popular movie critic, held her audience *Spellbound* in room *Number*

Seventeen of the *Jamaica Inn*. She was delivering a lecture on the films of Alfred Hitchcock. One *Rich and Strange Psycho* kept heckling her, shouting in a *Frenzy*: "Your talk went *Downhill* with your first sentence! This is *Murder*! Are you sure your name isn't *Marnie*? Who's got a *Rope*? Do you think we're all *Young and Innocent*? You are for *The Birds*! Is this a *Family Plot* by *Mr. and Mrs. Smith* to hire *The Farmer's Wife*, a lady of *Easy Virtue* for this job? *I Confess*, it's gotta be *The Skin Game*, *Blackmail*, or *Sabotage*. Without a *Shadow of a Doubt*, you're so full of it, I *Suspicion* that I'll need a *Lifeboat* to get out of here!" The critic could stand it no longer. So she showed the man exactly *Vertigo* — in *39 Steps*, right out the *North by Northwest Rear Window*, through the *Torn Curtain*. Then, the outraged and furious critic quickly left the room, shouting: "*The Lady Vanishes*!"

• • •

A police detective who hated homosexuals was fired because he unjustly arrested many alleged perpetrators who he even suspected of not being "straight." He was obviously living by the motto: *another gay, another collar.*

•••

The political leader of a small foreign country was informed by his advisors that the military was about to overthrow his government. The advisors also said that if he resisted the takeover, it would result in a lot of bloodshed and pose great danger to him and his family. They told him, "**If the coup hits, bear it.**"

•••

A very expensive but sadistic practitioner of Swedish massage derived intense pleasure from hurting his patients during his strenuous treatments. You might say he was engaged in **painful enjoyment**. You might also call his practice **massage terrorpy**.

•••

A zoo veterinarian specializing in treating big cats developed a safe method for trimming the nails on a lion's feet. He gently massaged them first to get the lion purring and in a good mood. He called this procedure **four-paw play**.

• • •

When the chemistry student was perplexed over why he produced a green solution instead of the blue one that the lab experiment called for, his professor remarked, **"What shows up dost confound."**

• • •

What do you call it when a spoiled, ungrateful child spreads false rumors about his father, when he can't have everything he demands? **Papagander**.

• • •

To get her way, a spoiled brat usually succeeded by going into a sobbing fit. When this didn't work, she burst into a fit of rage. To shut her up, her parents often gave in to one of these tantrums and let her have what she wanted. You see, she had remembered her parents telling her that "if at first you don't succeed, try, try again." In her case, she cleverly switched gears from **out of the crying plan and into the ire**.

• • •

A progressive school of dentistry introduced a unique course to its students. It consisted of teaching hypnotic techniques in combination with mild drugs as an alternative to injected anesthetics. This would induce complete absence of pain during extreme dental procedures. When asked by a friend how the professor teaches this, the student replied, "He **trains in dental medication**."

• • •

In trying to teach birth control to a vastly over-populated Third World country, the Public Health Missionary's mission was not to condemn the country, but to turn it into a **condomnation**.

•••

Every time a certain baseball pitcher lost a game, he would go into an uncontrollable rage, throwing things around the locker room and breaking a lot of the equipment. After a few too many of these outrageous performances, his manager called him into his office and said, "Look, son, you're a very good pitcher. But, even the best pitchers lose a game now and then. You've got to stop these destructive fits of temper after every loss. I'm warning you: **if you can't stand defeat, get out of the pitchin'.**"

•••

One of the pandas in a Chinese zoo developed an intense fondness for sweet potatoes. If he didn't get one every day with his usual diet of bamboo shoots, he would jump around in a frenzy, grunting and moaning. So the zookeeper made sure they always had a good supply of these vegetables. Otherwise, they had to endure the inevitable **pandamoaniyam**.

• • •

What did the farmer say when he found out that his daughter was planning to sneak off to get married to an unsuitable suitor? "Sorry to **squash** your **date** to **leek** off with that **bad-apple, has-bean, dead-beet lemon** who has no **celery** — but you just **plum cantaloupe!**"

• • •

What do you call an aged, dim-witted, alcoholic hobo who got swindled by his smarter hobo buddies? **Bum-booze-old**.

• • •

Penelope, a competitive swimmer, had very hairy legs. So, for the big swim meet, she decided to shave her legs in order to shave a fraction of a second off her time. Apparently, it must have worked. Penelope won her race by just one one-hundredth of a second! Shortly thereafter, she spent the day at the beach, but forgot to put sun block on her legs. The result was a bad sunburn on her naked, hairless legs. When she returned home, her mother remarked, "**A Penny shaved is a Penny burned.**"

• • •

When a group of battered ladies arrived in Reno for divorces from their abusive husbands, it was **a site for sore wives.**

• • •

Dripping wet wood should not be used in your fireplace. You should **let weeping logs dry**.

• • •

What do you call a porous marriage that becomes a nightmare for both spouses? **Holey dreadlock.**

•••

One July evening, a member of King Arthur's Round Table had a dream, during which he formulated an evil plan to overthrow his boss. It could be described as **A Midslumber Knight's Scheme.**

•••

When the owners of sled-dog teams in Alaska got to arguing endlessly about whether or not their huskies would run faster if given periodic snacks during their runs, instead of just one big meal a day, it was just a case of **Mush Ado About Noshing.**

•••

Back in one-room schoolhouse days, a flexible twig soaked in herb juice was said to have the power to inflict the same pain on naughty students with fewer strokes. In other words: **A switch in thyme saves time with pungent to fit the crime**.

•••

Every day, a man watched his neighbor taking her rapid morning walk past his house. When she started to appear with a walking stick, he got curious, because she was breezing by much faster with it than when she was without it. One day he asked her, "How come you are walking so much faster now that you are using a walking stick?"

She replied, "I use the stick to push off with at every other step, and that gives me my new whirlwind speed. That's why I call this stick my **hurrycane**."

•••

After several criminals had escaped to Reykjavik after hijacking armored cars for a lot of money, their haven became known as **Heistland**.

• • •

What do you call the golfer's disease that causes putts to constantly rim the cup and not drop in? **Liprosy**.

• • •

A new waitress dropped a stack of expensive china, and the restaurant owner yelled, "Get your butt out of here! You're fired!" It was a **DishAssStir**.

• • •

What do you call an intellectually challenged Southern debutante who pumps iron? A **dumb belle**.

• • •

What did the pro wrestler say when his opponent did a 360-degree, head-over-heels flip, before knocking him down and pinning him to the mat? "Wow! That was **some assault!**"

• • •

Concerned patient: "Why does my back feel like a lumpy board?"
Punny chiropractor: "Maybe because it's made of **knotty spine**."

• • •

Mrs. Teller, a long-time resident of a retirement home, was informing the newly hired Director of Dining Services about the worst complainers in the dining room. "Mrs. Oyl," she said, "has very crude ways of constantly criticizing the food here. And Mr. Steers, a real jerk, criticizes everything on his plate, even before he tastes it. We call these two troublemakers **'Crank Case'** and **'Beef Jerky.'**"

Answers on Page 123.

PUNZLE #1
When a very successful gambler mislaid his special pair of "loaded" craps cubes, with which he cheated many an unwary "sucker," he wrote a poem called:

P_ _ _ _ _ _ _ _   L_ _ _

PUNZLE #2
What is another good two-word definition of "horse sense"?

S_ _ _ _ _   I_ _ _ _ _ _ _ _ _ _ _

51

PUNZLE #3
How would you describe a lady who, in the middle of summer, wears a very expensive full-length sable coat to an informal bridge party?

F_ _ F_ _ _ _ _ _

PUNZLE #4
What are Native American moving men in Warsaw known as?

T_ _ _ _ P_ _ _ _

PUNZLE #5

What was the nickname of the minister who was criticized for his overly-long sermons, and who, instead of constantly checking his Timex, cut short his sermons whenever he observed some of the congregation dozing off or looking bored?

F _ _ _ _ W _ _ _ _ _ _

PUNZLE #6

How would you describe a novice skier who gets "folded up" on a very steep ski slope?

T _ _ _ _ _ _ _ _

PUNZLE #7
What's another way of saying that the biggest and strongest cows come down with diseases first?

T _ _ B _ _ _ _ H _ _ _
C _ _ _ _ _ _ _ T _ _ G _ _ _

PUNZLE #8
What was crooner Crosby's assistant called?

An U_ _ _ _ B_ _ _

54

PUNZLE #9
What do you call a spineless man who indulges in uncontrollable seven-day binges?

A W_ _ _ S_ _ _ _ _ _

PUNZLE #10
What do you call your sister's daughter who is so pretty that she causes comment wherever she goes?

A C_ _ _ _ _ _ _ _ _ _ _ _ N_ _ _ _

PUNZLE #11
What do you call a Madison Avenue ad man who stands among sunken treasure while diving in the deepest part of the Chesapeake?

T _ _ M _ _ I _ T _ _ B _ _
C _ _ _ _ _ _ L _ _ _

PUNZLE #12
What do you call a pleasant little Greenland town that never gets warmer than five degrees below zero?

A N _ _ _ _ _ _ _

PUNZLE #13
What do you call a playboy who dates famous women and jilts them as soon as his name is coupled with theirs in the society columns?

A F_ _ _ _ D_ _ _ _ _ _

PUNZLE #14
What do you call female Oriental carhops who work near "Old Faithful" in Yellowstone National Park?

G_ _ _ _ _ G_ _ _ _

PUNZLE #15
On January first, what did the zoo keeper post on a sign in front of the cage of a contented African antelope?

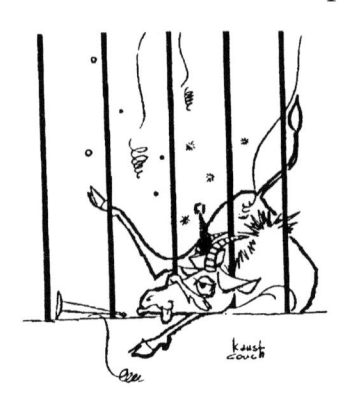

H_ _ _ _ G_ _ H_ _ _!

PUNZLE #16
Every April, when an old prospector finds gold dust by sifting sediment in his backyard stream, what did he call this process?

S_ _ _ _ _ G_ _ _ _ _ _ _

PUNZLE #17

When a man gains weight because he participates too heavily in the office Coke-and-cake break, what would he be justified in blaming it on?

T_ _ C_ _ _ _ T_ _ R_ _ _ _ _ _ _ _

PUNZLE #18

When the department store security guard apprehended a little boy with a just-stolen red metal toy soldier in his fist, his report read that he caught the boy how?

L_ _ _ H_ _ _ _ _ •••

Little Nellie had an awful temper and was always looking for a fight. When her classmates teased her, she "exploded" like a land mine and sometimes had to be restrained. That's how she got the nickname **ScrapNel**.

• • •

What do you call three intense, action-packed suspense movies — all scripted by the same writer and all dealing with the same general theme? A **thrillogy**.

• • •

On the day before Christmas break, the very attractive high school principal walked into the cafeteria in the midst of a food fight and was struck on the cheek by a flying bread ball. The local paper found out about it and wrote this headline for the story: "Pretty principal gets kissed by **missiledough**!"

• • •

Legend has it that in 16th-century England, the King of the Britons made frequent trips alone to spy on the Saxons, who were about to invade England. He always sent back written messages to his Knights of the Round Table, to report his findings. However, the joints in his fingers had become so swollen that one time he couldn't send a message. His Knights were so worried that they sent a note to him, which later became the name for his affliction, "**Arthur Write Us.**"

• • •

Every year, ballroom dancing holds its biggest competition in the U.S. to determine which couples are the most expert in spinning around on the dance floor. This event is so important to the contestants — many coming from all over the globe — that it has come to be called **The Whirl Serious**.

• • •

A man extremely allergic to bee stings was very upset when a beehive appeared in a tree near his house. He got a meat cleaver, climbed the tree, and chopped off the branch supporting the hive, which fell into the stream below. When his wife saw what had happened, and the hive floating away down the stream, she said, **"Cleaving is bee-leaving."**

• • •

In the pseudo-science of spiritualism, a theory holds that if an evil spirit male ghost is foolish enough to love an evil spirit female ghost, this romance must be broken up immediately by a ghost of higher authority. In other words, **a ghoul and his honey are soon thwarted**.

• • •

A very smart and shrewd businessman wanted a client to sign a contract that was very one-sidedly favorable to himself. So he got his client tipsy on many glasses of sherry, while fast-talking him into signing the contract. It was a clear case of **the mind leading the wined**.

• • •

A well-dressed lady snagged her beautiful Harris plaid jacket on her car door on the way to a high-society party. Luckily, she was traveling with a friend who was an expert seamstress and able to repair the damage on the spot, so she could attend the party in good shape. Gratefully thanking her seamstress friend, she said, "**A rend in tweed is a rend in need.**"

• • •

What do you call a charlatan spine doctor from Egypt? A **Cairoquacktor**.

• • •

After a lady of easy virtue had imbibed copious quantities of a wormwood liqueur, she began to think deeply and remorsefully about her wasted life. You might say that **absinthe makes the tart go ponder.**

• • •

A burglar heard that a church in town had just acquired some very valuable accessories for its altar, and decided to break in and steal them. He made a big mistake; he invited two other "baddies" to help him. They agreed that the items belonged to whoever grabbed them first. They jimmied the lock on the church door and broke into the closet where the altar items were stored. Immediately, they all spied a beautiful tapestry that was made from gold thread. All three of them grabbed the tapestry at the same time, and tried to wrest it away from the others. In the process, the tapestry tore in half. The moral: **Too many crooks spoil the cloth.**

• • •

It is rumored that in some Southern states, if you order the least expensive funeral, you might get one of the mortuary's "second-shift" limousines, which have been known to break down on the way to the cemetery. So, if you ever have to plan a funeral, make sure you **don't book a "shift" hearse in the South.**

• • •

What is the title of a song about a text book on ranching, left on the kitchen stove? **"Tome on the Range."**

• • •

The manager of a baseball team was excited about one of his new pitchers because he had an awesome fastball. But, his curveball didn't break sharply enough to fool the better hitters. He told the youngster that if he expected to pitch a successful, complete 9-inning game, he really needed to improve his curve. After working hard with the pitching coach, the player finally developed a superb, sharp-breaking curveball. Soon thereafter, he pitched a winning, complete game, with his curve working to perfection. His manager congratulated him "You see, my boy, **ball's swell that bends swell.**"

• • •

A child psychologist once formulated a theory about young children so terribly spoiled by their parents that they can never work hard at any task. This theory, simply stated: **"A botched tot never toils."**

• • •

When little Johnny come home from the playground filthy, his father said, "Who gave you all that mud? The **boggyman?**" Johnny's father believed in **making the pun-ishment fit the grime**.

• • •

The mother of twin boys couldn't understand why one of her sons was so messy, while the other one was just the opposite. Her husband told her to stop worrying about it, that some people are just born one way or the other. And that in the case of the boys, **"You've got to take the litter with the neat."**

• • •

Two neighbors had underground heated coils installed in their driveways to keep the snow and ice off in the winter. They employed different contractors to do the jobs. After the first freezing rain, neighbor number one promptly fell on the ice in his driveway. Neighbor number two didn't fall, because his driveway was completely free of ice. This only goes to prove that **the proof of the footing is in the heating**.

• • •

What do you call a bank clerk who moonlights by reading palms, while humming "Misty," "Stardust," "Linda," and "Dark Eyes"? A **fourtune teller**.

•••

If you were to strap a handgun onto an animated, marinated cucumber — thus creating a pistol-packing pickle — what animal would your action remind you off? An **armadillo**.

•••

What animal does your father's sister's electric blanket remind you of? An **ant-heater**.

•••

A Shakespearean actor was about to deliver the famous soliloquy in an outdoor performance of Hamlet, when he saw two rather large flying insects alight in his wig. Concerned that they might be the stinging kind, he inadvertently changed the opening line just a tad, **"Two bees, or not two bees, that is the question."**

•••

An old whaling sailor was instructing one of his novice seamen on the art of tying knots in harpoon lines. He warned that if the knots are not perfectly tied, they will foul up the coiling of the lines, which can cause the harpoon to be errantly launched. He summed up his lesson with this admonition: **"A botched knot never coils."**

• • •

When a professional panhandler, an avid reader of Ernest Hemingway, was asked if he could really make a decent living by begging, he showed himself to be a pretty good **punhandler**, too, by replying, "Yes, indeed. I **Fare Well with Alms**."

• • •

A very young firefly came upon a picnic table covered with breadcrumbs. Every time he landed on it to enjoy the delicious morsels, his mother kept nagging him, "Stop alighting on that table. You should be up in the air practicing lighting up your body." So, the baby firefly kept flying back and forth from table to sky so frantically, that after a while, he **didn't know whether he was crumbing or glowing**.

• • •

When a pianist went snorkeling in Hawaii, he wore two pairs of denims to protect himself from the sharp coral. However, a large wave washed him against the coral with such force that it tore a gash through both pairs of his bluejeans and gave him a nasty cut on his leg. When he reached the beach and saw the damage, he broke into a sardonic smile, because he thought of a slightly different title for the Gershwin piano piece that he was to perform in concert that evening: **"Ripsodeep in Blue."**

• • •

A recently downsized family man in Florida needed money to pay his bills and buy

Christmas presents for his kids. He took a part-time job picking grapefruit for a gourmet citrus fruit club. He was to be paid by the piece, but each had to be perfect. As he picked the fruit, he kept a mental count of the number of grapefruit he had picked each day, and calculated how much money he was making. At the end of the week, he figured he had made quite a sizeable sum. He was shocked, however, when his paycheck was only about half of what he had expected. He found out later that only half of the fruit he had picked was good enough to be sent out to the gourmet customers. The lesson he learned from this was: **"Don't count your pickins before they're dispatched."**

• • •

A judge threw out a suit for damages when he observed that each of the stories of the two litigants were obviously false, when two witnesses each revealed the true contradictory facts. It was a simple case of justice: **A lie for a lie and a truth for a truth**.

•••

It is rumored that legislation is in the works to support the legal growing of industrial Cannabis Sativa, which has less than .3% THC, the psychoactive component of marijuana. It can then be used to produce oil, flour, paper, canvas, textiles, fuels, paint, varnish, building materials, plastics, and, of course, rope. If New York State were to be a major grower of the plant, it would then be known as the **Hempire State**.

•••

A commercial raiser of weasels, in order to save a few dollars, fed his animals a poor grade of food. The consequence was that his animals developed weak eyes and runny noses as a result of their lack of proper nutrition. As a result, pet shops wouldn't accept his sick animals. The moral in this case: "**Runny is the snoot of all weasels.**"

•••

A bar in a very upscale neighborhood posted this sign: "We tolerate no fights, serve beer only in bottles, and prohibit smoking anywhere on the premises." They could have said it a lot shorter: "**No tiffs, cans, or butts.**"

•••

What do you call a pair of great-tasting candies made in the shape of human molars? A **toothsome twosome.**

•••

What do you call a beautiful rose blooming at the base of the most famous structure in Paris? An **eyeful flower.**

•••

Dickens, like many mid-Western towns, holds a pumpkin-seed-spitting contest every year to determine who can spit the seeds the farthest. In the latest contest, two past-champion participants did so well, that after comparing past performances all over the region, the promoters announced that the two Dickens' "spitters" had each broken the world distance record for pumpkin-seed spitting. The local newspaper's editor, who had studied English literature in college, heralded this accomplishment with this headline: **Great Expectorations in Dickens!**

• • •

A sailor was awakened by a loud scraping noise that came from the side of the ship near the water line. When dawn came, he peered out to see what was making the noise, and saw a huge, horribly scary giant squid trying to climb on board. It was truly **the fright at the bend of the gunnel**.

• • •

On the morning of the 1988 Super Bowl, a group of football fanatics got stoned at a pregame tailgate party. They got to arguing so intensely about which team was going to win that a terrible fight broke out. It took a dozen cops to break up the fight and haul the banged-up, knocked-out potheads to jail. Years later, this unfortunate event was still known as **"The Great '88 Stupor Brawl."**

• • •

During a local golf tournament, a young man's caddie tried to help his golfer by moving his ball from the edge of the rough into the fairway. When an official asked the caddie if he had moved the ball, he said, "No, sir, this is where it landed." The young golfer spoke up and said, "Yes, I do believe my caddie moved the ball a bit, and I deserve a penalty stroke." This occurrence could be summarized as: **a lie for a lie, and a youth for the truth.**

• • •

A nutrition-minded chemist developed a product that replaced lost sodium from hot weather perspiration, and which would not affect blood pressure. He felt that hypertensive athletes would flip over this product, which he called, "**Summersalt.**"

• • •

An English literature student, taking an open-book exam on *The Canterbury Tales,* got so exasperated with the difficulty of the questions that he threw the book out of the classroom window. The teacher, when he saw the book sailing over the campus, said, "Look, students, there goes the classic **Flying Chaucer!**"

• • •

What do you call that frantic period at the end of the year when you send cards, shop for presents, go to lots of parties, and decorate trees — all the while in a confused state of mind? The **hollydaze.**

• • •

An over-reactive mother went into a tirade when her baby daughter accidentally tipped over a nearly empty glass of pineapple juice on the kitchen table. She was **making a fountain out of a Dolespill.**

• • •

Many years ago, in a small European kingdom, the King had usurped much too much power for himself. When he died, the Ministers got together and passed a law that would prevent the new King from exercising the same unfair power his predecessor had wielded. They called this new law, **"The Fair Reign Check."**

• • •

An animal hospital was quite suddenly overloaded with nearly six dozen male cats — all badly deformed with rickets. The resident veterinarian, a hopeless punster, began to sing one of the songs from *The Music Man*, with a slight alteration to its title: **"Seventy Sick Tom Bones."**

•••

During the Spanish Inquisition, a notorious jailer-torturer invented a devilish, vice-like device that he used to inflict excruciating pain to the thumbs of his prisoners. He was so infamous for his cool cruelty that when another equally heartless torturer emerged on the scene, this newcomer was described as **cruel as the screwthumber**.

•••

A family of lions came upon a tree that had a dead antelope precariously hanging over one of its branches, probably dragged up there by a tiger intending to come back for it later. As the lions were gathering around the tree, trying to decide which one was going to climb up to bring down the feast, a stiff breeze came up and the antelope fell to the ground, whereupon the lions had a nice free meal. The moral: **Pride goeth before a fall**.

•••

A psychiatrist's patient was so fearful of so many things that it infected his personality and caused him a great deal of stress. The shrink summed up his case like this: **"Dread is the staph of strife."**

•••

A city guy retired to a little country farm, where he found himself in a constant battle with the grass and the soil — mowing and cultivating. He called it **mower-till combat**.

•••

Brilliant law student: What are you writing? And why are you using purple ink?
Not-so-brilliant law student: Our professor wants us to construct an iron-clad contract that is perfect "to a *T*" and will be valid forever. And he wants it in purple ink.
Brilliant law student: That's strange. Did he really specify all that?

<u>No-so-brilliant law student</u>: Yes. He said, and I quote from my notes, that the contract must be good **"in purple to a *T*."**

• • •

A scientist with a one-track mind had dedicated himself to producing a source of nuclear power without the danger of working with radioactive materials. He developed a large, synthetic, inverted cone with an ultra-fine iridium sieve on the small end. His idea was to slowly pour a special mixture of non-radioactive ingredients along the sides of the cone. This mixture would hopefully generate a safe form of nuclear power when it emerges from the sieve and through a chemical transformer. He was so single-mindedly focused on making this experiment work that you might say he had **funnel fission**.

• • •

When Noah's wife saw what a wonderful big boat her husband had made in order to survive the coming flood, she remarked, "What **a beautiful work of ark!**"

• • •

A girls' college basketball coach had two star players: Nellie (6'5") and his daughter Hyacinth (6'11"), both centers. Near the end of the last quarter of a very important game, both his stars were one foul away from fouling out. He needed a win, so he put both of them in the game at the same time. He figured that if one fouled out, the other would come through to score the winning points. He was determined to win "**come Nell or Hy daughter!**"

• • •

PUN-GHOULIES:
What's the weed that zombies are most allergic to? **Ghouldenrod.**

What's the fastest pace of a zombie horse? A **ghoulup.**

What's the name of a zombie's favorite composer? **Morton Ghould.**

What do you call a zombie's overshoes? **Ghouloshes.**

What's a zombie's favorite stew? **Ghoulosh.**

What do you call a female zombie who marries a male zombie just for his money? A **ghouldigger.**

What do you call a zombie who guards a hockey net? A **ghoulie.**

What's the name of the little girl zombie who visited the house of the three bears? **Ghouldie-Locks.**

What do you call a real hip zombie? A **ghoul dude.**

What's a zombie's favorite mustard? **Ghoulden's.**

What do you call a mystical religious zombie leader? A **ghoulru.**

What's the organ most often removed along with a zombie's appendix? The **ghoulbladder**.

What's a zombie's favorite pet? A **ghoulfish**.

What do you call a male zombie's main squeeze? His **ghoulfriend**.

What's the name of the H-shaped structures at both ends of zombie football fields? **Ghoulposts**.

What do you call the zombie practice of over-dramatizing something? **Ghoulding the lily**.

What does a male zombie call his indispensable female secretary? **My ghoul Friday**.

What do you call a zombie who is easily duped? **Ghoulable**.

What's a zombie's favorite book? *Jonathan Livingston Seaghoul*.

What's a zombie's favorite song? **"My Ghoul Sal."**

How do zombie politicians find out which zombies are most popular? With a **Ghoulup Poll.**

What's a zombie's favorite drink? **Ghoulade.**

Die-mens are a ghoul's best friends.

• • •

A famous bishop was to perform a special religious service, which included the ringing of the church tower bells. The local pastor was worried because the sexton who rang the bells was often drunk and not very dependable. So, when the service was about to start and the bells were to be rung, the pastor's worst fears were realized. The sexton, obviously under the influence, was seen staggering up to the bell tower. Everyone waited nervously to see if he would, indeed, make it to the top of the tower and ring the bells. The suspense involved in this regular procedure was such that the sexton was known as the **Cliffclanger**. In this case, however, after the sexton had reached the top of the tower and pulled the bell rope, he had a fatal heart attack. The entire episode was described in the local paper as "**The Tragedy of the Stiff Clanger.**"

• • •

The Daughters of the American Revolution needed to raise a lot of money for one of their philanthropic projects. In searching for an individual to head up the project, they finally appointed Frederick Johnson, the husband of one of their members, to conduct the fund-raising effort. One DAR member, when she heard about Mr. Johnson's appointment to this demanding job, remarked to Mrs. Johnson, "I see you've **cast your Fred upon the Daughters.**"

• • •

A farmer was concerned and perplexed when some of his ducks and chickens were disappearing from his barn without a trace. A neighbor came by and offered this "helpful" advice: "If you are sure it's not a fox that's taking your foul, you must be losing them to a ghost of some sort. I would guess it's the work of a **poultryheist**."

• • •

A very fastidious owner of an upscale restaurant was very proud of the wonderful pies his expert baker made. He always watched as the pies came out of the oven. If any of them were not absolutely perfect, he would ring a bell, and those imperfect pies would be put aside for consumption by the staff. The pies that met with his standard of perfection were known as **"No Bell Pies."**

• • •

A wealthy psychic owned a bottle of priceless 75-year-old scotch, which he vowed never to open. He said that when he died, he would come back as a ghost to guard that bottle. A year later, he did die, and when his son tried to open the bottle, the psychic's ghost did, indeed, appear and scare his son away. That ghost became a local legend and was known as **"The Spirit of 76."**

• • •

The high-roller craps shooter at a big casino had just made his seventh winning pass in a row, letting his winnings ride with each roll of the dice. He then decided to test his luck just one more time. He blew on the dice and exclaimed, "Come seven! Come eleven!" Just before he threw the dice, an excited spectator shouted, "Look, everybody! **The Diceman Cometh**!"

• • •

A racehorse owner nicknamed three of his horses "The Three Musketeers," because they looked so much alike, and because Alexander Dumas was his favorite author. Another horse in this stable was a big winner because he had the ability to squeeze through a pack of horses on the track, as though he were coated with grease.

Every time that horse won a race, the owner gave him his favorite treat, a bucket of canned vegetables. He named this horse, of course, **"The Mount of Del Monte Crisco."**

• • •

A manufacturer of factory whistles test-marketed his whistles in several different quarries that previously had no efficient way to advise workers when to stop work. The shrill sound of this particular whistle caused rockslides in every quarry where the whistles were tested. All of which proves that **there are toot slides to every quarry.**

• • •

Two men, shipwrecked on an island that they thought was deserted, were starving. One said, "Let's get some bacon from that bacon tree over there."

The other man said, "Are you delirious? There's no such thing as a bacon tree!" The first man strode over to the tree in question to prove him wrong, but soon he staggered back, his body covered with arrows.

"You were right," he stammered. "That was a **ham bush**!"

• • •

When a fortune-teller asks you for your birth date and then predicts that your house will burn down, her words constitute a **horrorsmoke**.

• • •

PUN WITH FROGS:
What do frogs sit on when they are in the woods? **Toad stools**.

What is a frog's favorite soft drink? **Croaka-Cola**.

After a spring rain, the neighborhood frogs would gather around the newly formed pool to drink the fresh water. They called that period their **Hoppy Hour**.

Visitor: Isn't this the county that used to be overrun with jackrabbits?
Resident: Yes, but that was a long time ago. Now, it's frogs. Instead of being known as Rabbit Country, we're being called **Ribbit Country**.

A little girl caught a frog in the woods, and remembering a fairy story, kissed it in the hope that it would turn into a prince. Instead, the frog shot out of her hand like a rocket and disappeared into the woods. What the little girl didn't know was that the frog was a unique species known for its speedy jumping ability. That's why it was called a **missletoad**.

The frogs in a little southern town were getting very upset with the large number of drivers speeding over the dirt roads, killing a lot of them as they attempted to cross the road. So furious were they that thousands of them got together one day, and massed themselves onto one section of the road. This stopped traffic for a long period of time, killing a lot more of them in the process. This was the headline in the local newspaper reporting this unusual occurrence: **"Toad Rage Brings Local Traffic to a Croaking Halt."**

A tragedy had just happened to one of the Florida frog families. A great blue heron had gobbled up all the baby frogs that had disobeyed their parents and wandered off into the swamp. If they had listened to their parents and had **toad the mark**, they wouldn't have **croaked** before their time.

A bunch of frogs was conducting the annual "Ribbit" Contest. One of the group, a big bullfrog, won the contest almost every year. This time, however, one of the other frogs remarked that the Big Boy wasn't in very good voice during the practice warm-up session, remarking that he sounded like he had a human in his throat. "Yes," said another frog. "Today, **he's not what he's croaked up to be.**"

• • •

When a show-off actor steps under the bright movie lights, one is reminded of a standard American breakfast: **ham and kleigs**.

•••

In football, the jarring impact of the ball-carrier and the tackler, as the former smashes into the end-zone for a touchdown, could be called a **goalision**.

•••

Where do cheese manufacturers send their smelly, spoiled merchandise? To **limboburger**.

•••

A boy, surprised by his irate mother while standing near the cookie jar, the contents of which he had just consumed, is truly **behind the ate bowl**.

•••

A rowdy delinquent, who is an expert performer on the ice and is well liked by his buddies, could be called **a hood skate.**

• • •

A great deal of fishing and hunting in extremely cold and nasty weather can easily result in a case of **gills and beaver.**

• • •

A beautiful girl in the kissing booth at a Christmas Day bazaar is a **very kissed miss** (and a Happy New Year).

• • •

The patriotic leather-factory worker, after a losing fight with his strong, lady-Coast-Guard wife, is **"The Spar-Mangled Tanner."**

• • •

As he drank the poison, the Oriental gentleman yelled, **"Cyanara!"**

• • •

If an army of aliens from one of our nearest planets were to invade the Peach Tree State, it would be called **Martian through Georgia.**

• • •

A magnificently engraved bugle was presented to the army's finest bugler. He used it only on special occasions to assemble the troops for full-dress review. This instrument came to be known as the bugler's **musterpiece.**

• • •

After our first President fell on some ice outside an inn in Trenton, New Jersey, this sign was posted in the establishment's window: **"Washington slipped here!"**

•••

Why is a high-fashion dress designer like a high-powered automobile? Because they both need plenty of **galsolean.**

•••

What did the mountaineer call the revenuer who discovered his moonshine apparatus and destroyed it? A **stilljoy.**

•••

What was George Gershwin's favorite fish story? "**Porgy and Bass.**"

•••

An electric device used to strip fur from rabbits makes such a terrifying noise, it's called a **hare razor.**

•••

A sailor wearing a size-10 hat went to the hospital suffering with fluid on his brain. It was a clear-cut case of **water on the bulkhead**.

•••

What do you call a hen that lays square eggs? **Eggcentric**.

•••

A slapstick comedian who achieved fleeting popularity by continually getting hit by a pie in his face, was characterized by an entertainment weekly as **a flush in the pan**.

•••

A person who is always quick to criticize the remarks of others is said to speak **on the slur of the comment**.

•••

Two men removed the wall that separated their farms. They felt that neighbors should be trusting and **fencey-free**.

• • •

How is a confused bullfighter who falls into a cement machine like a confused figure of speech? They're both a **mixed mataphor**.

• • •

A stern, strict English teacher, so preoccupied with her diagrams that she spends most of her time in front of the blackboard, could certainly be called **slate-faced**.

• • •

What do you call an optometrist's assistant who cleans his patients' eyes before he examines them? An **eyegienist**.

• • •

Father's walking stick, which stood in the corner as a constant warning against bad behavior, or else it would be used in a temper-tempest of punishment, was referred to by the children as father's **worrycane**.

• • •

A cow, which hates to be hooked up to the milking machine, looks at it in **udder fastenashun**.

• • •

A three-year-old child, who terrorizes the neighborhood by recklessly driving his little electric motorcar on the sidewalk, is truly a **motorious totrodder**.

• • •

A retired railroad employee, who every day visits train yards because he's "nuts" about train engines, is driven to it by a **loco-motive**.

• • •

What the spider caused Miss Muffet to do to her breakfast, when he sat down beside her, coincided with her opinion of said spider: **floor the curds**.

• • •

A young actor was doing a scene for a motion picture in which he was portraying a dashing, devil-may-care swordfighter in the Errol Flynn tradition. The director noticed that the tights he was wearing bore the famous trademark of Nike, a serious anachronism for this period piece. From that time on, this actor had the nickname "**Swooshbuckler**."

• • •

<u>John</u>: Hey, Jim, guess what? I'm going to a High Tea tomorrow!
<u>Jim</u>: Really? I thought those High Teas were strictly for stuffy old women.
<u>John</u>: I did, too. But the notice advertising this

one said they were going to have scones and **strumpets**. And if that's not a misprint, that's my cup of tea!

• • •

What do you call an evil fellow who repeatedly flirts with wealthy women and lies to them in order to get them to lend him money — and after he gets the money, takes off and is never heard from again? A **hit and run coniver**.

• • •

After a shrink had his first session with a young girl who had obviously been traumatized by an overly dominating mother, and seemed to be in a permanent zombie-like state, the doctor summarized the case in his notebook in one word: "**Mommyfied**."

• • •

When William Shakespeare was a teenager, he had the habit of leaving scraps of his writings all over the house. One day, when scribbled pages from *King Lear* and *Hamlet* were strewn on all the chairs and tables, his mother said resignedly, **"Where there's a Will, there's a play."**

• • •

A professor of American literature had a son and daughter who were polar opposites. The daughter was an early-riser, who always got down to breakfast on time. The boy, however, had to be awakened several times before he would arrive at the breakfast table — always late. One morning, however, the boy surprised everyone. He woke up by himself and appeared at the table at the same time as his prompt sister. His astonished father proclaimed, "Wonders never cease! **The son also rises.**"

• • •

The waitstaff at an independent-living retirement facility made a mistake and provided half-size paper napkins to one of the resident tables. Since all the other residents were provided with full-size napkins, one of the diners with the small napkins looked around at the next table with the full-size napkins and proclaimed in a loud voice, "I guess we are the **Halfs**, and you are the **Half-Nots!**"

• • •

Shirley May, a Georgia college student, on the first day of class, raised her hand and asked permission to go to the rest room. The professor said, "You **surely may**." She said, "Yes. That's my name, but may I go to the rest room?"

• • •

Late one evening, during the tax season, a tired and irritable man was poring over his 1099s and various voluminous records, trying to figure out how much he was forced to pay to the government. In the middle of his calculations, he chanced to look out the window at a bright, star-studded sky. Suddenly, he laughed and broke out singing, "The stars at night, are big and bright, **deep in the hurt of taxes**."

• • •

The local judge in a small country town was not adverse to cracking a joke or a pun when announcing a sentence. After the jury had convicted a local perpetrator of his latest crime, the judge made this sentencing speech. "I see by your rap sheet that you have been accused and convicted of shoplifting 144 items from stores throughout this county. Therefore, I am **centurying** you to 100 days in jail and 144 hours of community service to make amends for your **gross** behavior, and fining you a **grand** total of $1000 to be paid to the court in 20 days to settle the **score**."

• • •

After a naughty little boy had done something particularly bad, it was his mother Helen who administered the punishment, usually a sound spanking. One evening, when his father returned from work, he saw his son sobbing hysterically and holding his sore bottom. Since he didn't approve of this kind of severe punishment, he couldn't resist saying, loud enough for his wife to hear, "I see **you've been to Helen back.**"

• • •

In describing his tiny new cubicle to a friend, the newly hired computer trainee said, "Yes, you could call it a hole-in-the-wall. But I like to call it my private **orifice.**"

• • •

What do you call a disabled comedian who delivers his corny jokes from a wheelchair? A **sit-down comic?** Or a **ham on a roll?**

• • •

Everybody knows that young geese are called goslings. But what are old geese called? **Geesers**.

• • •

The proud father instructed all his kids to shout like mad when his eldest boy did great things during the team's final basketball game. He knew that several scouts for the pros were in the stands and he wanted them to pay strict attention when his boy stole the ball, shot his patented three-pointer, and slam-dunked while doing a 360 in mid-air. In other words, he wanted his kids to **make horray while the son shines.**

• • •

Where do cyber-spiders spend their leisure time? At their **web sites**.

• • •

A young boy was trying to provoke his older sister into an argument by jumping around and yelling at her. She would have none of it. When he kept bothering her, she said to him, "Stop dancing around with those stupid statements. I will not argue with you, because **it takes two to tangle**."

•••

During rehearsal, the high school Music Director was beside himself. The cymbal player in the band was constantly coming in at the wrong time with his cymbal clash. The young man maintained that his entry point gave a much better effect and that he wouldn't play it as written. When the Music Director was asked by the Principal why he fired the young musician from the band, he replied, "It was a simple case of **cymbal disobedience**."

•••

In a little town in New Jersey, near where George Washington was reputed to have been with his troops, there is a very old inn that was quite a tourist attraction, because the owners claimed that George Washington had, indeed, spent the night there. Hence, the big sign out in front that proudly stated, "Washington slept here!" Down the block, the owner of an equally old historic building that housed a combination saloon and general store, decided to get some publicity for himself. Since he speculated that, while there, Washington must have stepped into his establishment to quench his thirst, have a meal, buy some provisions, and carry them back to the inn — the proprietor erected his own large sign out in front of his place of business. This one proudly stated, "Washington stopped, sipped, supped, shopped, and **schlepped** here!"

• • •

The church elders were outraged when they discovered that Grace, their female minister, was suspected of taking money out of the collection plate for her own personal use. In a special meeting to discuss this matter, one of the elders said, "This is a **fine kettle of fishiness**. It's **disGraceful**! I'm really not surprised. I was worried about her when I saw those expensive clothes she always wore. And stealing the collections? **I wouldn't put it pastor!**"

• • •

A deadbeat father, incarcerated for his failure to pay alimony and child support, was assigned to hose down the prison bathrooms. That's why all the other prisoners called him **The Floorflusher**.

• • •

A teenage girl was very grumpy because nobody had asked her to go to the junior prom. So she sulked on the sofa the entire day and did nothing but watch TV. When her father observed this behavior, he said to her, "So, I see we have a **grouch tomato** living with us today!"

• • •

A man who loved puns had a brother who hated them. One day, just before Halloween, the pun-lover issued this challenge to the pun-hater, "I'm going to tell you ten short puns, and I'll bet you'll like at least one of them." After he told his brother ten outrageous puns — all on ghosts — he said, "OK, tell me, is there a chance that you thought one out of ten of these ghost puns is funny?"

"No," said his brother, **"Not a ghost of a chance. No pun in ten did!"**

• • •

In a Bible study class, the students were discussing the significance of what happened to Adam and Eve in the Garden of Eden. One male student maintained that the downfall of man was not Adam's fault, because he believed Eve when she told him (prompted by the serpent) that it was OK to eat from the Tree of Life. A female student angrily said: "Do you mean to say that the sinfulness of mankind was all the fault of a woman?"

"Yes, I do," shot back the young man. **"How do you like them apples?"**

• • •

Johnny's teacher told his parents that their son was having a lot of trouble in English class, dealing with punctuating his compositions correctly. She said, "Whenever he tries to add punctuation to his reports, he goes into a sort of stupor, and literally becomes **comma-tose**.

• • •

A U.S. Senator drove the other Senators crazy by always peppering his addresses with a series of word plays and puns. His colleagues called this undignified display **Capitol pun-ishment**.

• • •

A Dutchman named Hans had three sons, all of whom he named after himself, like George Foreman, who named all of his sons George. One day, the Dutch sons, who worked as handymen in a factory, were called upon by the foreman (**no relation to George**) to replace a hard-to-reach fluorescent bulb that one of the other workers could not replace alone. The three brothers, together, were able to do the job in a jiffy. The foreman then remarked, "**Many Hans make light work.**"

• • •

An elderly gentleman, just after his annual physical, was being warned by his physician that he was still seriously overweight. The doctor asked him, "What are you doing to keep sugar, fats and cholesterol-loaded foods in your diet at bay?"

The gentleman's wife said (pointing at his protruding belly), "He's keeping them at bay all right — at his **bay window**."

• • •

A fishing guide was famous for being able to take his clients to an exact spot on Moosehead Lake in Maine, where they would invariably catch a lot of fish. His secret was that, years ago, he had gone scuba diving in the lake and discovered a large cleft on the lake bottom, where a large number of lake trout always congregated. Another interesting fact about this guide was that he was an extreme manic-depressive. Out fishing, he was always in the manic state, whooping and hollering every time he or his clients caught another trout. So he became known as **"The Maine-ic Fissureman."**

• • •

A young computer programmer named Dorothy was extremely talented in her work at a high-tech company. She spent all her breaks and lunch periods playing on the Internet. She was very snooty about her capabilities, and also resented her being kidded about all the time she spent surfing the Net. In addition, she was a very crude, coarse, and common person. When some of the other employees got together one day to discuss her, one guy said, "I've got an idea on how we can call her by a derogatory name, which she will think is a compliment. Her name is Dorothy, right?

And she's a computer whiz, right? And she's a very common person, right? So let's call her **Dot Com**."

• • •

A teenage shoplifter promised her new girlfriend that if she would help her steal some CDs from a music store, she would cut her in on some of the loot, and it would be a lot of fun. Her horrified new friend replied, "You mean you want me to **sin and share it?**"

• • •

Two buddies who loved to bet on the horses at the neighborhood racetrack were discussing their favorite all-time race horses. They finally decided that Secretariat was the best. "Yes," said one to the other. "**The feeling is pari-mutual, and you can bet on it.**"

• • •

A nursing home had so many of its patients falling down and breaking their bones that they posted signs all over the facility: "Haste Makes Waste!" But one of the nurses had a better idea. She suggested changing the signs to read: **"Haste Makes Breaks!"**

• • •

Juanita and Tyler Gonzales, sister and brother, were called by their parents and friends, "Juan" and "Ty." One day, shortly after new neighbors had just moved in next door, Mrs. Gonzales called the kids in for lunch in her usual way: "Ty! Juan!" The new neighbors thought that was odd. Why would Mrs. Gonzales shout "Taiwan" — when she knew they came from Mexico? And much later, when the kids were teenagers and cutting up a bit at a beer party, their friends would joke, **"Look at them Ty Juan on!"**

• • •

Little Jimmy was upset because he couldn't jump over the low hedge in his backyard, like his older brother could. When his mother heard him crying, she said to him, "Don't worry, Jimmy. In just a little while, you'll be able to do it. **As you shall grow, so shall you leap.**"

• • •

A visitor to a Southern Evangelistic church saw the minister preaching in his wheelchair, at the top of his Bible-thumping powers. He said to his pew-mate, "Now that's what I call a genuine **Holy Roller!**"

• • •

A very naughty boy took great delight in taking a sickle and cutting down his neighbor's sugar cane field. When the boy's mother saw what he was doing, she shouted to her husband, "That's your son! Stop him! He's out there again **razing cane!**"

•••

A very old lady was steadily becoming more and more forgetful. She was still able to read, however, and she was very fond of Agatha Christie's mystery books, particularly those featuring lady detective, Miss Marple. She owned a lot of these books, but she kept misplacing them, never being able to locate the one she had been reading last. When the doctor asked the old lady's daughter how her mother was getting along, she said, "Same old story. **She's losing her Marples.**"

•••

The patient in the hospital's emergency room had taken a nasty fall on his rear end when he tripped on a bad crack in his driveway. When the doctor asked the nurse about the nature of the patient's injury and what had happened, she replied, **"Assfault!"**

•••

When an airline passenger, who happened to be an architect, noticed that one of the stewardesses had a more-than-generous posterior, he remarked to his seat-mate, "Now, that's what we in the trade would call a **flying buttress!**"

• • •

A book that contains a complete collection of the Sherlock Holmes detective stories, in which Sherlock never overlooks the most minute of clues, could be called a **fine-sleuth tome**.

• • •

William Shakespeare was reputed to be a real tightwad. He was always suspicious of the greengrocer's scales. He hated to be cheated by rigged scales, so he always brought along his own scales whenever he bought produce at the local markets. That's why his friends, when they saw him in the market, said, **"Wherever there's a Will, there's a weigh."**

• • •

Soon after a world-famous dancer insured her legs for $1 million, she had an accident that left her legs permanently paralyzed. She died of a heart attack a few months later, whereupon her husband inherited the money that the insurance company had paid for the accident. The newspaper headline read: Dancer's Husband Gets Million-Dollar **Leg-acy**.

• • •

The Administrator of a hospital, a born punster, was very worried. In just one week's time, a great number of patients had come down with skin infections and food poisoning from undercooked meat. So he called an emergency conference of all his medical and kitchen personnel. His memo to them was headlined: **Staph Meating**!

• • •

A little country town needed a new recreation center for their teenagers. The old building was dangerous, because it was literally falling apart. In order to pay for a new structure, the Town Council had an idea: charge a fee to anyone who wanted to participate in demolishing the old building. It worked! The whole town turned out with sledgehammers and pickaxes and had a great time knocking down the old building. And a great deal of money was collected for the new recreation center. The local newspaper headlined the story: **Fun Razing a Smashing Success**!

• • •

A patient needed a very delicate operation immediately to save his life. However, the operation was a new procedure, and very few knew how to perform it. The surgeon on duty telephoned the surgeon who had developed the revolutionary procedure, and luckily, the latter said that he had printed detailed instructions for the operation, and that he would fax them immediately. The result was another triumph for technology.

Following the faxed directions to the letter, the surgeon performed the operation and saved the patient's life. The surgeon had indeed received **The Fax of Life**.

• • •

Two construction workers on their lunch break were discussing what they did on their former jobs. The first man said he always had a **driving ambition** to operate an eighteen-wheeler, but soon got tired of that job. The second man said he used to have a dirty job: cleaning out portable toilets. Upon which his friends said, "Boy, what a **stinkin' offal** job that was!"

• • •

A beauty shop owner was frantic. Her only other hairdresser, in addition to herself, quit on Wednesday, and there were a lot of customers with reservations for Saturday, which she couldn't handle by herself. So she quickly placed a help-wanted ad in the local paper. On Friday, she had three applicants to interview, but they were all terrible. So, that evening, she was in a horrible mood, because she had to call a lot of her customers to cancel their appointments. Her husband, noticing her bad mood, said to her: "What's the matter?" She replied, "I've had a **bad hire day!**"

• • •

What does a hot-coals-walker get when he loses his nerve? **Coal feet.**

• • •

A hell-fire preacher was telling his congregation that all of them were sinners. In winding up his sermon, he shouted (while rapidly pointing up and then down): "You all better **shape up or ship down!**"

• • •

The king of a small European country had an ongoing property dispute with Carl Krantz, the king of the neighboring country. Letters didn't have any effect, so the outraged king went to see King Krantz face-to-face at the gate of Krantz' palace. He said to the guard, "Take me to your leader, Krantz." When the guard hesitated, the king added, "You know, **your leader Krantz— the big cheese** here."

• • •

Remember folks:
A DAY WITHOUT A PUN
IS A DAY WITHOUT PUNSHINE!

PUNZLE ANSWERS

1. Pairodice Lost
2. Stable Intelligence
3. Fur-fetched
4. Totem Poles
5. Flock Watcher
6. Telesloped
7. The Burley Herd Catches the Germ
8. UnderBing
9. Week Sipster
10. Conversation Niece
11. The Man In The Bay Channel Loot
12. Niceberg
13. Flame Dropper
14. Geyser Girls
15. Happy Gnu Here!
16. Spring Gleaning
17. The Cause That Refleshes
18. Lead Handed